Improve Clear Thinking

Turning Ordinary Moments into Extraordinary Results

Sandra J. Cline

Copyright Note

© Sandra J. Cline 2024

Overview

Are you tired of feeling stuck in a rut? Do you crave a life filled with joy, creativity, and endless possibilities? Say goodbye to boring and hello to greatness with "Improve Clear Thinking: Turning Ordinary Moments into Extraordinary Results."

This groundbreaking book offers a unique method to unlock your full potential. With proven strategies and practical insights, you'll learn how to transform mundane jobs into exciting chances for growth and discovery. But that's just the beginning.

Here's what you can expect:

Master the art of clear thinking: Learn how to quiet your inner critic and beat self-doubt. Discover how to turn chaos into clarity and make confident decisions.

Ignite your creativity: Say goodbye to the "blank page" problem and hello to endless ideas. You'll learn how to spark new ideas, solve problems, and create like never before.

Build healthy relationships: Discover the power of emotional intelligence and learn how to control your feelings with ease and grace. You'll develop deeper relationships and build a more fulfilling life.

Welcome vulnerability: Break free from limiting ideas and accept your true self. You'll learn how to be more real, build strength, and live a life of meaning and purpose.

Make a lasting impact: With useful tools and insights, you'll be prepared to leave a good mark on the world around you. You'll be a force for good, making a real difference in your neighborhood and beyond.

This isn't your normal self-help book. It's a game-changer, created to help you unlock your real potential and live an amazing life. You'll learn to see the world in a new light and turn ordinary times into amazing results.

So why wait? The magic you seek is already within you. With "Improve Clear Thinking," you'll learn how to unlock it and watch your life change before your eyes.

Are you ready to step into a brighter, more brilliant future? Then grab this book and get started today. Your best life is waiting.

Author message

In today's fast-paced and rapidly changing world, the ability to think clearly and make smart choices is more important than ever. The book "Improve Clear Thinking: Turning Ordinary Moments into Extraordinary Results" is an important resource for anyone looking to improve their thinking skills and achieve success in their personal and professional lives.

Drawing on decades of study and experience in the field, the author provides useful strategies and techniques that readers can use to beat cognitive biases, avoid common thinking mistakes, and make better decisions. With clear, concise writing and relatable examples, this book is available to readers of all backgrounds and levels of experience.

Whether you're a business leader, a student, or simply someone who wants to improve your thinking skills, "Improve Clear Thinking" is an important guide for handling the complex challenges of the modern world. With the knowledge and tools given in this book, readers can learn how to turn ordinary moments into amazing results and achieve their goals with confidence and clarity.

Inspiring message

As someone who has studied and researched the art of clear thinking for years, I can confidently say that Improve Clear Thinking: Turning Ordinary Moments into Extraordinary Results is a must-read for anyone looking to enhance their cognitive abilities and achieve greater success in both their personal and professional lives. With practical tips, real-world examples, and engaging tasks, this book is a thorough guide that will take you on a journey to develop your critical thinking skills and improve your decision-making processes. By the end of this book, you'll have the tools you need to turn your ordinary moments into amazing results. So, if you're ready to take your thinking to the next level, then I highly recommend picking up a copy of Improve Clear Thinking today.

TABLE OF CONTENTS

Introduction

Unlocking the Extraordinary in the Ordinary

Imagine a world where every moment, no matter how ordinary, contains the potential for extraordinary results. Where the seemingly mundane becomes the impetus for creativity, innovation, and personal growth. This is the world that awaits you when you unleash the power of straightforward thinking.

Have you ever felt trapped in a rut, living on automation, and yearning for more? Perhaps you've experienced moments of frustration, pondering why success seems elusive while others seem to effortlessly achieve their goals. The truth is, that the seeds of extraordinary results are often concealed within the ordinary moments of our existence. It's just a matter of recognizing them, nurturing them, and leveraging their potential.

This book is your guide to unlocking the secrets of straightforward thinking. We'll embark on a journey together, investigating the foundations of this powerful tool, identifying the thinking traps that hold us back, and cultivating the habits that empower us to progress forward. You'll learn how to:

- [ ] Decipher the concealed messages in ordinary experiences
- [ ] Recognize and surmount your inherent biases
- [ ] Master the discipline of observation and critical thinking
- [ ] Develop a mental model for success
- [ ] Break free from negativity and emotional triggers
- [ ] Transform ordinary situations into extraordinary outcomes

Through compelling stories, practical exercises, and actionable insights, this book will provide you with the knowledge and tools you need to unleash your complete potential. Whether you're a seasoned professional attempting to reach new heights or an individual yearning for a more fulfilling life, clear thinking is the key to attaining your objectives.

So, get ready for this transformative journey, turn the page, and unleash the extraordinary within.

Part 1:Foundational Elements of Clear Thinking

Chapter 1: The Power of Ordinary Moments

Have you ever contemplated the latent possibilities that lie within the quotidian occurrences that comprise your existence? Moments that appear inconsequential are frequently disregarded in our hasty progress through the day. Disregarding the richness of quotidian experiences, we pursue grandiose aspirations and fantasize about pivotal moments that will propel us to success.

Unusually, it is in the most quotidian of moments that extraordinary outcomes frequently originate. Creative breakthroughs, impassioned pursuits, and extraordinary accomplishments can be propelled by the ostensibly ordinary, routine, and mundane. Think, for instance, of the accidental inventions that have revolutionized history, the chance encounters that have led to enduring alliances, or the silent reflections that have spawned innovative ideas.

Ordinary moments are like fertile soil, waiting to be cultivated. These circumstances provide an exceptional prospect for introspection, development, and exploration. We can acquire valuable insights, recognize patterns, and connect seemingly unrelated connections by observing the minutiae of our daily lives. Our minds can activate a store of potential during moments of solitude, such as those spent on a morning stroll, engaged in routine duties, or even just before bed.

To begin, an appreciation of the impact of ordinary moments: consider the following simple exercise:

1. Take a moment to pause and reflect on your day. What were some of the ordinary instances you experienced?
2. Try to recall any details that stood out to you. What images, sounds, odors, or sensations did you notice?
3. Now, examine yourself: How could these ordinary instances be interpreted as potential seedlings for growth? What insights, inspiration, or opportunities might they hold?

Additional exercises

Exercise 1: The 5 Senses

1. Take five minutes to sit silently in a comfortable environment. Close your eyes and focus your attention on your five senses: sight, sound, fragrance, flavor, and touch.
2. What do you see? Is there anything that stands out to you, even if it seems insignificant at first glance?
3. What do you hear? Are there any sounds that you typically shut out, but that you can now appreciate with focused attention?
4. What do you smell? Is there a particular fragrance that elicits a memory or emotion?
5. What do you taste? Can you detect the subtle flavors in your cuisine or drink?
6. What do you feel? Pay attention to the sensations of your body against your attire, the chair beneath you, or the air on your skin.

Exercise 2: Journaling

1. Dedicate ten minutes each day to writing in a journal about your ordinary moments. Reflect on your experiences, thoughts, and feelings without judgment.
2. Look for patterns and connections between seemingly unrelated events. Do any insights emerge from your reflections?
3. Identify potential opportunities for development or creativity within your ordinary experiences. How can you use these insights to enhance your life?

By cultivating this mindful awareness, you begin to see the world through a new lens. You discover the concealed narratives within the mundane and unleash the potential for extraordinary results. As you cultivate this approach, **you'll uncover yourself**:

1. Developing a deeper appreciation for the present instant.
2. Becoming more attentive and attuned to your surroundings.
3. Unearthing unforeseen opportunities for creativity and innovation.

4. Connecting seemingly unrelated experiences to form a more coherent understanding of the world.

Application:

Integrate practices for appreciating ordinary moments into your daily routine. Take regular mindful breaths, initiate conversations with acquaintances, and appreciate the minor delights of ordinary life.

Use the power of ordinary moments to enhance your creativity and problem-solving. Brainstorm ideas while taking a walk, find inspiration in everyday objects, and connect seemingly unrelated concepts to inspire innovation.

Share the delight of appreciating ordinary moments with loved ones. Engage in shared experiences, express gratitude for each other's presence, and cultivate a life bountiful in modest, meaningful moments together.

Bear in mind that the extraordinary frequently conceals itself in the mundane. Through cultivating mindfulness, decelerating one's pace, and fully engaging in the current moment, one can access the potential for innumerable mundane occurrences to undergo profound changes.

Utilize this heightened sense of gratitude for quotidian occurrences as a framework to perceive the world. Consider life an infinite canvas of opportunities for connection, happiness, and personal development. Embrace the extraordinary voyage that unfolds in front of your eyes at each instant that appears inconsequential.

Task

Choose a specific everyday task you often perform on autopilot (e.g., making coffee, or taking a walk). For one day, actively slow down and pay close attention to all the sensory details and feelings involved with this action. Notice what you learn and how your experience changes.

Create a "gratitude jar" or journal. Throughout the day, write down small things you're grateful for, focused on ordinary times and everyday blessings. Rereading these posts can shift your viewpoint and improve your well-being.

Plan a "date with yourself" to fully savor an everyday action you enjoy. Go stargazing, cook a delicious meal, or indulge in a relaxing bath, but give your full attention to the experience without distractions.

Challenge yourself to find beauty in the everyday. Capture pictures of ordinary items or scenes with a new viewpoint, write a poem about your daily commute, or create a piece of music inspired by the sounds of nature.

Share your stories of appreciating ordinary times with others. Inspire them to see the beauty and promise in their own everyday lives, starting a talk about mindfulness and finding joy in the present.

Questions for reflection:

Can you remember a recent ordinary moment that suddenly connected with you? What tiny features or interactions made it special?
Do you tend to rush through your days, missing the potential importance of everyday moments? What methods can you adopt to become more present and mindful in your day-to-day life?

How do you currently celebrate or recognize the beauty and importance of ordinary moments? Consider journaling, expressing thanks, or making artistic images of these times.

Have you recognized any limiting beliefs that prevent you from fully enjoying the power of everyday moments? Perhaps beliefs about needing grand events or successes to feel satisfied. Explore how these ideas might be harming your happiness and well-being.

What real steps can you take today to turn an ordinary moment into something extraordinary? This could involve participating in mindful conversation, savoring a meal with purpose, or connecting with nature through a mindful walk.

Notice, That the extraordinary often resides within the mundane. By slowing down, paying attention, and embracing the present moment, you can activate the transformative power of innumerable commonplace experiences.

Let this appreciation for commonplace moments become a lens through which you view the world. See life as a canvas replete with infinite opportunities for connection, delight, and personal development. Embrace the extraordinary journey that transpires right before your eyes, in every insignificant instant.

The enchantment resides in recognizing that the extraordinary is not reserved for special occasions or spectacular exploits. It's woven into the very fabric of our daily existence, waiting to be discovered by those who choose to see it. So, open your senses, suppress your inner critic, and embrace the power of ordinary moments. You may just be astonished by the extraordinary results they yield.

Chapter 2: The Brain and its Biases

Welcome to the intriguing world of the brain, the most complex and potent organ in the human body. It is the seat of our thoughts, emotions, perceptions, and decisions. Yet, despite its remarkable capabilities, the brain is not without its limitations. One of the most significant challenges we face in our pursuit of clear thinking is the inherent bias within our neural pathways.

These biases are profoundly engrained in our minds and have evolved over millennia to serve a critical purpose: survival. They enabled our ancestors to make quick decisions in a perilous world, often based on limited information and time. However, in the modern world, these same biases can lead to misinterpretations, misunderstandings, and ultimately, flawed decisions.

Here are some of the most common biases that can hinder clear thinking:

Confirmation bias: We are inclined to favor information that confirms our existing beliefs and disregard evidence that contradicts them. This can contribute to a narrow-minded perspective and an inability to see situations objectively.

Availability heuristic: We judge the likelihood of an event based on how readily examples spring to mind. This can lead to overestimating the risk of uncommon events and underestimating the risk of prevalent ones.

Anchoring bias: We rely too significantly on the first piece of information we receive when making a decision. This can lead to us being persuaded by irrelevant information and making suboptimal choices.

In-group bias: We favor individuals and groups that we identify with and are more likely to trust their information. This can lead to discrimination and prejudice against those outside our group.

Self-serving bias: We are inclined to claim credit for successes while blaming external factors for failures. This can prevent us from learning from our errors and enhancing our performance.

While these biases are endemic to our biology, they are not insurmountable. By understanding how they operate and actively working to overcome them, we can cultivate a more rational and objective approach to making decisions.

Here are some strategies for overcoming cognitive biases:

Seek out diverse perspectives: Surround yourself with individuals who have diverse backgrounds and viewpoints. This will enable you to challenge your assumptions and see things from a different angle.

Question your first impressions: Don't rush to conclusions based on limited information. Take the time to compile all the facts before formulating an opinion.

Be cognizant of your emotional state: Emotions can distort our judgment. Try to identify and manage your emotions before making essential decisions.

Practice critical thinking: Learn to analyze information objectively, identify logical fallacies, and distinguish facts from opinions.

Embrace continual learning: Continuously expand your knowledge base and develop new skills. This will enable you to become more flexible and adaptable in your thinking.

Questions for reflection:

Can you identify a situation where your reasoning was likely influenced by a cognitive bias? How did it affect your decisions or judgments?

Do you believe you're generally aware of your own biases? What strategies could you implement to become more cognizant of your mental shortcuts and assumptions?

How comfortable are you challenging your own beliefs and perspectives, even when confronted with conflicting evidence? What measures can you take to cultivate intellectual humility and receptivity to new information?

Have you witnessed instances where someone else's prejudices led to misunderstandings or unjust treatment? How can you advocate for critical thinking and responsible communication in your personal and professional interactions?

Do you believe it's possible to thoroughly eliminate our biases, or simply become more aware of them? Explore the concept of bias management and its potential for enhancing our decision-making and interpersonal relationships.

Tasks:

Research and understand common cognitive biases. Choose five that resonate with you, and create flashcards or visual representations to remind yourself of their potential influence on your thinking.

Engage in perspective-taking exercises. Imagine a situation from someone else's viewpoint, contemplating their background, values, and potential biases. This can help you identify your own biases and broaden your understanding.

Participate in frank and respectful discussions with individuals from diverse backgrounds. Actively listen to their perspectives and challenge your assumptions when challenged by conflicting viewpoints.

Implement critical thinking strategies when evaluating information. Analyze the source, identify potential biases, and consider alternative explanations before forming conclusions.

Practice bias-aware communication. Be mindful of the language you use and avoid perpetuating stereotypes or assumptions. Focus on comprehending and acknowledging diverse perspectives instead of asserting your own as the absolute truth.

Application:

Use your knowledge of biases to enhance your relationships. Seek common ground and respectfully communicate your needs while acknowledging the potential influence of biases on both parties.

Become a champion of critical thinking in your community. Encourage others to query assumptions, analyze information objectively, and value diverse perspectives.

Apply bias management strategies to your decision-making processes. Take measures to acquire all relevant information, consider potential biases, and consult with diverse individuals before making important choices.

Remember, everyone is susceptible to biases. This encompasses you. By perpetually learning, actively reflecting, and engaging in open communication, we can endeavor to mitigate the negative impact of biases and cultivate a more informed and understanding world.

Let your awareness of biases become a catalyst for personal and societal growth. Embrace the ongoing voyage of challenging assumptions, expanding your comprehension, and contributing to a more inclusive and equitable future.

By comprehending and addressing the biases inherent in our brains, we can unleash the full potential of our minds and make better judgments in all aspects of life. The journey to clear reasoning begins with awareness and self-reflection. By actively working to overcome our cognitive limitations, we can establish a foundation for a more fulfilling and successful existence.

Chapter 3: Building a Mental Model for Success

What if you could construct a mental model, a personal blueprint that guides your thoughts, decisions, and actions toward attaining your goals? This model, customized to your unique values, aspirations, and strengths, would serve as a powerful instrument for navigating the complexities of life and accomplishing remarkable results.

Imagine a ship navigating the immense ocean. Without a defined trajectory, it would drift aimlessly, vulnerable to the vagaries of wind and tide. Similarly, without a well-defined mental model, we risk being thrown about by external forces, succumbing to distractions, and losing sight of our true purpose.

Building a robust mental model is an essential step in the journey toward clear thinking and success. It involves:

Defining Your Values And Goals: What are the fundamental values that govern your life?

What are your long-term and short-term goals?

How do your objectives align with your values?

Taking the time to address these questions provides a firm foundation for your mental model. It helps you prioritize your actions and make decisions that are consistent with your innermost desires.

Developing A Development Mindset: Embrace challenges as opportunities for learning and development.

Believe that you can develop your skills and abilities through effort and perseverance.

View setbacks as transient obstacles, not enduring limitations.

A growth mindset fosters resilience and adaptability, essential qualities for navigating the inevitable challenges and setbacks that life sends our way.

Cultivating Self-Awareness:

Become aware of your strengths, limitations, and biases. Understand how your emotions and beliefs influence your decisions.

Practice self-reflection and learn from your experiences.

Self-awareness empowers you to make conscious choices and take control of your mental state. It enables you to identify areas for improvement and devise strategies to overcome your limitations.

Building A Knowledge Base: Continuously study and acquire new knowledge in your selected field.

Seek out different views and question your assumptions.

Stay informed about current events and trends that may impact your objectives.

A robust knowledge base provides the foundation for informed decision-making. It equips you with the necessary instruments to analyze situations objectively and make sensible judgments.

Visualizing Your Success:

Create a vivid mental image of yourself attaining your objectives.

Imagine the emotions, sensations, and experiences associated with success.

Use this image as a source of motivation and inspiration.

Visualization is a potent instrument for programming your subconscious mind for success. By vividly envisioning your desired outcome, you increase your chances of attaining it.

Taking Action: Develop a plan of action with concrete steps to attain your objectives.

Set realistic deadlines and hold yourself accountable.

Track your progress and celebrate your achievements.

Taking action is the most crucial element of developing your mental model for success. It translates your aspirations into tangible results and propels you towards attaining your ambitions.

Remember, your mental model is a dynamic entity. It should evolve and adapt as you learn and grow throughout your existence. By continuously revisiting your values, objectives, and strategies, you ensure that your mental model remains pertinent and effective in guiding you toward remarkable success.

Here are some additional tips for building a strong mental model:

Read inspirational accounts and biographies of successful individuals.

Engage in activities that promote mental well-being, such as meditation and exercise.

Connect with a mentor or coach who can provide guidance and support.

Seek out opportunities to acquire new abilities and develop your talents.

Application:

Integrate your ideal mental paradigm for success into your daily decision-making. Ask yourself how each choice correlates with your values, contributes to your long-term objectives, and helps you cultivate the qualities you believe are essential for success.

Share your mental model for success with trusted colleagues and family members. Discussing your vision can solidify your commitment, encourage positive feedback, and develop a support system that aligns with your aspirations.

Be flexible and adaptable as you construct and refine your mental paradigm for success. Life's journey is full of unexpected turns, and your definition of accomplishment may evolve. Embrace learning, development, and continuous adjustments to ensure your model remains pertinent and empowering.

Remember, your mental paradigm for success is a potent tool for shaping your existence. Choose it judiciously, nurture it incessantly, and let it steer you toward a fulfilling and meaningful journey

By investing in your personal development and cultivating a robust mental model, you equip yourself with the tools needed to navigate the challenges and opportunities of life. You empower yourself to make informed decisions, achieve your objectives, and ultimately, live a life of fulfillment and purpose.

Notice, that the journey to success is a marathon, not a sprint. Exercise patience, be persistent, and be committed to your growth. With dedication and effort, you can construct a mental model that becomes your compass, guiding you toward attaining extraordinary results.

Part 2: Recognizing and Avoiding Thinking Traps

Chapter 4: The Emotional Rollercoaster

Humans are emotional creatures. Our emotions impact our thoughts, choices, and actions. While emotions can be potent motivators and sources of inspiration, they can also be a significant obstacle to clear thinking. When we allow our emotions to usurp our discernment, we react impulsively, make irrational decisions, and ultimately hinder our ability to achieve our goals.

Imagine experiencing an emotional rollercoaster. One minute you're soaring high on the crest of a positive emotion like pleasure or exhilaration, and the next instant you're plummeting into the depths of sorrow, anger, or fear. This constant fluctuation can be exhausting and detrimental to our mental well-being and decision-making.

Here are some ways that emotions can negatively impact clear thinking:

Distorted perception: When we are emotionally aroused, we tend to see things through a distorted lens. We may exaggerate the importance of certain events, misinterpret others' intentions, and make decisions based on impulsive reactions rather than rational analysis.

Reduced cognitive flexibility: Emotions can restrict our focus and make us less receptive to new information or differing perspectives. This can lead to inflexibility in our thinking and hinder our ability to solve problems effectively.

Poor impulse control: When we are overtaken by strong emotions, we may struggle to control our impulses and act in ways that we later regret. This can lead to impetuous decisions, damaged relationships, and missed opportunities.

Fortunately, there are strategies we can use to manage our emotions and prevent them from hindering our clear thinking:

Identify your triggers: Pay heed to the situations and events that provoke strong emotions in you. Understanding your triggers can help you anticipate emotional reactions and develop coping mechanisms.

Practice mindfulness: Techniques like meditation and deep breathing can help you become more aware of your emotions and regulate them in the present. By observing your thoughts and feelings without judgment, you can acquire control over your reactions and respond thoughtfully instead of impulsively.

Reframe your thoughts: When faced with a challenging situation, attempt to reframe your thoughts more positively. This can help you regulate your emotions and maintain a tranquil and rational perspective.

Express your emotions healthily: Find healthy ways to express your emotions, such as talking to a trusted friend, journaling, or engaging in creative activities.

Bottling up your emotions can exacerbate the problem and lead to unhealthy coping mechanisms.

Seek professional help: If you struggle to manage your emotions on your own, consider obtaining professional assistance from a therapist or counselor.

Questions for reflection:

How comfortable are you acknowledging and navigating your emotions? Do you tend to suppress them, react reflexively, or approach them with inquiry and understanding?

Can you identify specific triggers that tend to send your emotions on a rollercoaster? Are they external situations, internal beliefs, or particular behaviors? Understanding your triggers can help you proactively manage your emotional responses.

What coping mechanisms do you currently use to cope with difficult emotions? Are they wholesome and effective, or do they sometimes lead to negative consequences? Reflecting on your coping strategies can help you make conscious choices about managing your emotions more productively.

Tasks:

Practice mindfulness exercises to become more aware of your emotions in the present. Take mindful breaths, focus on your somatic sensations, and name your emotions without judgment. This can help you acquire control over your reactions and make more conscious choices.

Create a "feelings wheel" or chart to visualize your emotional landscape. Categorize your emotions and investigate their nuances. This can help you comprehend how various emotions connect and how to navigate them effectively.

Develop healthy coping mechanisms for managing difficult emotions. Identify healthy alternative solutions, such as expressing yourself through journaling or creative endeavors, seeking support from loved ones, or engaging in physical activity.

Application:

Use your emotional awareness to enhance communication in your relationships. Express your needs and feelings assertively, attend actively to others' emotions, and practice empathy to create deeper connections.

Leverage your comprehension of emotions to make smarter decisions. Before making critical choices, acknowledge and consider your emotional state to avoid impulsive or regretful actions.

Become a champion for emotional intelligence in your community. Advocate for open dialogue about emotions, encourage responsible emotional expression, and promote tools and strategies for healthy emotional management.

Remember, the emotional turmoil is a natural aspect of the human experience. Embracing your emotions, understanding their triggers, and developing healthy coping mechanisms, you can navigate this turmoil with greater control and grace.

Let your emotional intelligence become a compass for navigating life's challenges and opportunities. Use your emotions as valuable information, leverage them for positive change, and allow them to guide you towards a more fulfilling and authentic voyage.

By comprehending the impact of emotions on clear thinking and developing strategies to manage them, we can better navigate the intricate world of our interior selves. We can learn to leverage the power of our emotions for positive transformation and prevent them from becoming obstacles to our success.

Remember, clear reasoning is not about suppressing your emotions. It's about comprehending them, managing them effectively, and using them to inform your decisions and actions thoughtfully and purposefully. By cultivating emotional intelligence, we can develop resilience, strengthen our relationships, and ultimately accomplish extraordinary results in all aspects of life.

Chapter 5: Ego & Identity: The Distorting Lens

Within each of us resides a complex entity: the ego. It's the part of our self that defines our sense of identity, molds our perceptions, and motivates our actions. While the ego plays a crucial role in developing self-esteem and guiding our behavior, it can also become a significant obstacle to clear thinking.

Think of the ego as a lens through which we perceive the world. This lens can distort our reality, amplifying our strengths and achievements while diminishing our weaknesses and failings. It can lead us to overestimate our abilities, make biased judgments, and become defensive in the face of criticism.

Here are some ways that the ego can hinder clear thinking:

Self-deception: The ego often protects us from uncomfortable truths by constructing a narrative that supports our self-image. This can lead us to disregard evidence that contradicts our beliefs and makes it difficult to learn from our errors.

Attachment to opinions: When our ego becomes invested in a particular opinion or belief, we become resistant to altering our minds, even when presented with compelling evidence. This can lead to closed-mindedness and lost growth opportunities.

Fear of failure: The ego dreads failure because it views it as a threat to our self-worth. This dread can paralyze us and prevent us from taking risks or venturing outside our comfort zone.

Competition and comparison: The ego flourishes on the comparison, perpetually seeking validation and confirmation of its superiority. This can contribute to emotions of envy, resentment, and unhappiness.

Fortunately, there are ways to overcome the limitations of the ego and cultivate clear thinking:

Practice self-awareness: Pay attention to your thoughts and identify how your ego might be influencing them. Be honest with yourself about your assets and weaknesses.

Seek feedback: Actively seek constructive feedback from others to acquire various perspectives and identify areas for improvement.

Embrace humility: Cultivate an attitude of contrition and be open to learning from others. Recognize that you don't have all the answers and that you can always learn and develop.

Focus on the present moment: The ego often dwells on the past or frets about the future. By focusing on the present moment, you can detach from your ego and see things more clearly.

Practice self-compassion: Be kind and understanding towards yourself, particularly when you make errors. Remember that everyone makes errors, and self-compassion is essential for learning and development.

By recognizing the limitations of the ego and actively working to surmount its negative influences, we can break free from the distorted lens it projects onto our reality. We can adopt a more objective and open-minded perspective, leading to clearer thinking, better decision-making, and ultimately, a more fulfilling existence.

The voyage towards clear reasoning is not about suppressing the ego. It's about understanding its function, recognizing its limitations, and learning to use it as a tool for development and self-improvement. By achieving a healthy balance between ego and self-awareness, we can navigate the complexities of life with clarity, wisdom, and grace.

Striking The Balance: Ego, Self-Awareness, And The Cost Of Ignorance

Maintaining a healthy balance between ego and self-awareness is crucial for achieving clear thinking and navigating life effectively. While a robust ego can provide us with confidence and motivation, an inflated ego can lead to arrogance, self-deception, and ultimately, negative consequences.

A robust ego is like a well-tuned instrument. It allows us to express ourselves, pursue our objectives, and contribute meaningfully to the world. However, when the ego becomes excessively inflated, it begins to distort our reality. We become preoccupied with our importance, oblivious to our shortcomings, and resistant to feedback.

Self-awareness, on the other hand, functions as a counterweight to the ego. It helps us see ourselves objectively, recognize our limitations, and learn from our errors. When we are self-aware, we are open to feedback, willing to adapt and change, and ultimately, more capable of attaining our objectives.

The cost of ignoring the need for this balance can be significant.

Individuals with an inflated ego often experience:

Damaged relationships: Their arrogance and lack of empathy can strain relationships with loved ones and colleagues.

Missed opportunities: Their resistance to feedback and their closed-mindedness can prevent them from learning and developing, leading to missed opportunities for advancement and success.

Internal conflict: The continual need to maintain a dominant image can be emotionally draining and lead to feelings of anxiety, insecurity, and discontent.

Impeded progress: Their inability to learn from errors and adapt can hinder their personal and professional growth.

Loss of credibility: Their arrogance and lack of self-awareness can erode the trust and respect of others.

Recognizing the signs of an inflated ego is essential for taking corrective action. **Some key indicators include**:

Exaggerating achievements and minimizing failures.

Being excessively sensitive to criticism and feedback.

Needing incessant acclaim and validation.

Having difficulty admitting errors and assuming responsibility.

Being disdainful of others' opinions and perspectives.

Constantly comparing oneself to others.

Questions for Reflection:

When have you encountered the ego creating conflict in your relationships? Did it manifest as a need for control, defensiveness, or a struggle for recognition? How did you address this conflict, and what could you learn from it?

Imagine removing the distorting lens of the ego for a moment. What qualities and values would define your authentic self? How might your perspective on life and relationships be different?

Have you observed instances where societal expectations or conditioning influenced your sense of self? How can you identify and challenge these external influences to reclaim your unique voice and identity?

Tasks:

Practice shadow work: Journal about your insecurities, anxieties, and negative characteristics. By acknowledging these aspects of yourself, you can integrate them into a more whole and authentic self-image.

Create a "values compass": Identify your fundamental values and personal principles. Use this compass to make decisions, prioritize duties, and navigate challenging situations with increased clarity and alignment.

Engage in creative expression: Paint, write, dance, or find another outlet to connect with your inner self and explore your authentic expression. Let your creativity guide you beyond the limitations of the ego and express your unique essence.

Application:

Practice mindful communication by focusing on active listening and empathy. Shift the focus from your narrative to comprehending the perspectives and experiences of others. This can help dissolve ego-driven barriers and establish stronger connections.

Set boundaries based on your requirements and values. Learn to say no to requests that deplete your energy or conflict with your priorities. Prioritizing your authentic self fosters respect and nurtures healthier relationships.

Celebrate your "imperfections": Embrace your idiosyncrasies, vulnerabilities, and unique perspectives. Remember, your faults and inconsistencies are not weaknesses, but rather the strands that weave the tapestry of your authentic self.

Inspire others to abandon the distorting lens of the ego. Share your journey of self-discovery and encourage open conversations about identity and authenticity. By normalizing vulnerability and self-exploration, we establish a space for collective development and acceptance.

Never cease investigating the depths of your being. This is a lifelong journey, and the rewards are bountiful. By continually stripping back the layers of ego and cultivating your authentic self, you pave the way for a life filled with purpose, connection, and profound personal fulfillment.

By cultivating self-awareness and seeking feedback from trusted sources, individuals can begin to identify and address these patterns. They can engage in practices like journaling, meditation, and mindfulness to acquire a deeper understanding of their thoughts, emotions, and motivations. Additionally, pursuing professional guidance from a therapist or coach can provide valuable support and tools for managing ego and cultivating self-awareness.

The voyage towards a healthy equilibrium between ego and self-awareness is an ongoing process. It requires continuous self-reflection, open-mindedness, and a willingness to learn and develop. By investing in this endeavor, we can unlock our full potential, accomplish greater success, and cultivate fulfilling and meaningful relationships.

The choice is ours: to remain confined within the confines of an inflated ego, or to embrace the path of self-awareness and unlock the extraordinary potential that resides within.

.

Chapter 6: Social Pressures: Conformity vs. Independence

Humans are social creatures. We are designed for connection and belonging, and as such, we are naturally susceptible to the influence of social pressures. These constraints, both real and perceived, can significantly impact our thoughts, decisions, and actions. While conformity can offer some benefits, such as fostering social cohesion and facilitating cooperation, it can also lead to a loss of individuality and hinder our ability to think for ourselves.

The classic Asch Conformity Experiment demonstrated the power of social pressure. Participants were asked to determine the length of lines, and even when they knew the correct answer, they often conformed to the incorrect majority opinion. This experiment emphasizes the inherent human tendency to follow the herd, even when it goes against our judgment.

here are some ways that social pressure can negatively impact clear thinking:

Limited perspective: When we conform to the expectations of others, we limit our ability to consider alternative perspectives and solutions. This can lead to groupthink, where individual creativity and critical thinking are suppressed.

Dread of rejection: The dread of being ostracized or derided can lead us to suppress our thoughts and beliefs to blend in. This can be detrimental to our self-esteem and sense of identity.

Loss of authenticity: When we consistently endeavor to conform to external expectations, we lose contact with our true selves and our values. This can lead to a sense of inauthenticity and disconnect from our interior world.

Inhibiting critical thinking: When we uncritically embrace the opinions of others, we fail to engage in critical thinking and make informed decisions based on our judgment and analysis.

Fortunately, we can develop strategies to resist negative social pressures and cultivate independent thinking:

Develop self-awareness: Recognize your susceptibility to social pressure and the ways it might be influencing your thoughts and decisions.

Practice critical thinking: Question your assumptions and beliefs, and don't be reluctant to challenge the status quo.

Seek diverse perspectives: Surround yourself with individuals who have diverse backgrounds and viewpoints. This will help you broaden your perspective and contemplate alternative solutions.

Develop strong personal values: By having a clear comprehension of your values and principles, you will be better equipped to resist pressure that contradicts them.

Practice assertive communication: Learn to express your opinions and beliefs confidently and respectfully, even in the face of disagreement.

Seek support from like-minded individuals: Surround yourself with people who value independent thinking and critical analysis. This can provide you with the encouragement and support you need to remain genuine to yourself.

The essential point to observe, cultivating clear thinking requires courage and individuality. It means being willing to stand up for what you believe in, even when it's controversial. By embracing independence and resisting the draw of conformity, you pave the way for a more fulfilling existence, replete with authentic expression and personal growth.

The choice lies before us: to succumb to the constraints of conformity and merge into the throng or to embrace independent thinking and forge our unique path. Let us choose the latter, and in doing so, unleash the extraordinary potential that resides within each of us.

Chapter 7: Inertia: The Enemy of Progress

We all confront the potent force of inertia, the tendency to remain in a state of rest or uniform motion. This applies not just to physical objects but also to our beliefs, routines, and behaviors. Inertia can be a formidable opponent in our pursuit of clear thinking and attaining extraordinary results.

Imagine attempting to push a hefty boulder uphill. It can be overpowering and discouraging, making it alluring to give up entirely. Inertia operates in much the same way, enticing us to remain in our comfort zones, resist change, and settle for the status quo.

here are some ways that inertia can hinder our progress:

Procrastination: We put things off until the last minute, averting the effort and discomfort of commencing something new.

Comfort zone: We adhere to familiar routines and behaviors, even if they no longer serve us.

Dread of failure: We avoid taking risks or venturing outside our comfort zone for the dread of making mistakes.

Lack of motivation: We struggle to find the energy and enthusiasm to surmount initial resistance and initiate action.

Negative self-talk: We tell ourselves stories about why we can't succeed, further reinforcing the sense of inertia.

Fortunately, there are strategies we can adopt to overcome the pull of inertia and propel ourselves toward our goals:

Set SMART goals: Define your objectives using the SMART framework: Specific, Measurable, Achievable, Relevant, and Time-bound. This helps break down larger objectives into smaller, manageable tasks.

Start small and develop momentum: Don't attempt to change everything at once. Begin with small, achievable tasks and progressively increase the difficulty as you gain momentum and confidence.

Break down the resistance: Identify the specific thoughts and feelings that are holding you back and confront them directly. Challenge your negative self-talk and replace it with empowering affirmations.

Create a positive environment: Surround yourself with supportive people who encourage your efforts and honor your achievements. Eliminate distractions and create a space conducive to focused work.

Reward yourself: Acknowledge and reward yourself for taking action and achieving milestones. This reinforces positive behavior and helps you stay motivated.

Seek accountability: Find a friend, family member, or mentor who can hold you accountable for your objectives. This provides additional support and helps you remain on course.

Focus on the progress: Instead of solely focusing on the final objective, celebrate your progress along the path. This helps you remain motivated and avoid becoming overwhelmed by the larger picture.

Practice mindfulness: Mindfulness techniques like meditation can help you become aware of your thoughts and emotions without judgment. This enables you to identify and address the fundamental causes of inertia before they sabotage your progress.

Here are some questions to reflect on to help you identify and overcome inertia in your life:

What are the areas in your life where you are experiencing inertia? Be specific and identify the duties or objectives you are postponing or struggling to achieve.

What are the thoughts and sentiments that are holding you back? Are you afraid of failure, overburdened by the task, or simply lacking motivation?

What are your current objectives and are they SMART? Are they Specific, Measurable, Achievable, Relevant, and Time-bound? Reevaluate your objectives to ensure they are clear and actionable.

What small measures can you take to surmount the initial resistance? Break down larger objectives into manageable tasks and focus on making progress, not attaining perfection.

Who can you rely on for support and accountability? Surround yourself with positive individuals who encourage your efforts and celebrate your achievements.

What are some strategies you can implement to combat negative self-talk? Practice mindfulness and replace limiting beliefs with empowering affirmations.

Do you reward yourself for your progress along the way? Acknowledge and celebrate your accomplishments, no matter how minor, to remain motivated and on track.

Are there any external factors contributing to your inertia? Identify and address any environmental or situational challenges that might be hindering your progress.

When was the last time you reviewed your goals and priorities? Regularly re-evaluate your objectives and ensure they still align with your values and aspirations.

Do you prioritize your well-being? Maintaining a healthy balance in your life, including sufficient sleep, exercise, and stress management, is crucial for overcoming inertia and building long-term momentum.

By reflecting on these concerns and actively addressing the fundamental causes of inertia, you can unlock the extraordinary potential that lies within you.

Overcoming inertia is not about achieving immediate results. It is a journey that requires perseverance, persistence, and a commitment to self-improvement. By employing these strategies and actively working to surmount the forces holding you back, you can break free from the grip of inertia and embark on a path toward extraordinary results.

The choice is yours: to remain stuck in the quagmire of inertia, or to find the courage and determination to accept change and push yourself towards a life of satisfaction and success.

Part 3: Cultivating Clear Thinking Habits

Chapter 8: Mastering the Art of Observation

Observation is the bedrock of straightforward thinking. It fuels our understanding of the world, influences our decisions, and ignites our creativity. By learning to observe with intention and awareness, we uncover a treasure trove of insights, hidden patterns, and unanticipated connections.

Imagine a seasoned detective piecing together the clues at a crime scene. They meticulously investigate every detail, no matter how minor or insignificant it may seem. Their trained eye notices subtle discrepancies, seemingly random objects, and even minor changes in behavior. By observing these details and connecting the links, they can solve the mystery and bring the culprit to justice.

Similarly, we can cultivate our detective-like skills by mastering the art of observation. This involves refining our senses, practicing mindful awareness, and developing a keen eye for detail.

Here are some key aspects of mastering the art of observation:

Sensory Awareness:

Sight: Pay attention to the hues, contours, textures, and movements within your environment. Notice subtle variations in lighting, expressions, and gestures.

Sound: Listen attentively to the various noises around you, from the faint whispers of the wind to the intricate melodies of a tune.

Smell: Take a moment to appreciate the diverse odors that come your way, from the revitalizing scent of rain to the comforting fragrance of a loved one's perfume.

Touch: Feel the textures of diverse surfaces, the warmth of a cup of coffee, or the tenderness of a feather.

Taste: Savor the complete flavor of your food, observing the delicate balance of sweet, sour, salty, and bitter elements.

Mindfulness: Be present: Focus on the present without getting lost in distractions or ruminating about the past or future.

Be non-judgmental: Observe without labeling or categorizing what you see, hear, or experience.

Be curious: Approach the universe with an inquisitive mind, asking questions and pursuing deeper understanding.

Active Attention:

Find patterns: Identify recurring themes, connections, and relationships between seemingly disparate elements.

Ask questions: Don't accept things at face value. Challenge your assumptions and pursue alternative explanations.

Challenge your biases: Be aware of your own biases and prejudices and actively search out information that contradicts your existing beliefs.

Conclude: Analyze your observations and draw logical conclusions based on the evidence you have gathered.

By cultivating these skills, we become more than mere observers; we become detectives of the everyday world. We begin to see beyond the surface, uncovering the concealed meanings and stories that reside beneath.

This newfound awareness empowers us to:

Make better decisions: By observing and analyzing situations with greater depth, we can make informed choices that are aligned with our values and objectives.

Solve problems creatively: By identifying patterns and connections, we can approach problems from new angles and develop innovative solutions.

Establish stronger relationships: By paying close attention to others' nonverbal cues and emotional states, we can nurture deeper connections and establish trust.

Become more adaptable: By observing how others navigate challenges and surmount obstacles, we can learn valuable lessons and adapt to changing circumstances.

Expand our knowledge and understanding: By observing the world around us with curiosity and intention, we can perpetually learn and develop, expanding our knowledge and understanding of the world.

Unveiling the Hidden World: Practical Steps to Master Observation

The road towards learning the art of observation isn't simply about passive awareness. It's a dynamic and interactive process that needs active involvement and deliberate practice. Here, we jump into **practical steps** you can take to improve your observing skills and unlock a better understanding of the world around you

CULTIVATE SENSORY AWARENESS:

Engage your senses intentionally: Start by focusing on one perception at a time. For instance, during your morning coffee, give close attention to the fragrance, the warmth in your hands, the subtle changes in color as the cream swirls, and the delicate noises of stirring.

Seek out sensory experiences: Immerse yourself in environments abundant in diverse sensory stimuli. Visit art galleries to observe textures and hues, attend concerts to appreciate the nuances of sound, or experience nature to feel the textures of leaves and the invigorating fragrance of fresh air.

Document your observations: Keep a sensory journal where you record your observations, noting down the details that stand out to each sense. This practice helps you refine your focus and strengthen your memory.

PRACTICE MINDFUL OBSERVATION:

Start with brief mindfulness exercises: Begin by incorporating brief periods of mindfulness into your daily routine. Focus on your respiration, somatic sensations, and the thoughts and emotions that arise. This cultivates a state of non-judgmental awareness, which translates into your observations.

Engage in meditative walking: Take a walk to observe your surroundings with full awareness. Notice the details you typically overlook, like the intricate patterns in leaves, the expressions of pedestrians, or the subtle changes in light and shadow.

Mindfully attend to conversations: Pay close attention not just to the words being spoken, but also to the tone of voice, body language, and interruptions between words. This can reveal concealed emotions, intentions, and unspoken messages.

DEVELOP ACTIVE ATTENTION:

Ask open-ended questions: Approach situations with inquiry and a desire to learn. Ask questions that encourage deeper understanding and challenge your assumptions. This helps you see things from diverse perspectives and uncover concealed details.

Look for patterns and connections: Pay attention to recurring themes, similarities, and relationships between ostensibly unrelated elements. This can lead to unanticipated insights and creative solutions.

Challenge your biases: Be cognizant of your preconceived notions and prejudices. Seek out information that contradicts your existing beliefs and actively challenge your biases. This enables you to observe the world with greater objectivity and clarity.

REFLECT AND ANALYZE:

Take time to reflect: After observing a situation or experience, take time to reflect on your observations. What did you notice? What surprised you? What concerns do you still have?

Connect the dots: Look for connections between your observations and derive conclusions. What does this tell you about the situation or the individuals involved?

Share your observations: Discuss your observations with others. This can help you acquire various perspectives and refine your understanding.

Questions for Reflection:

What are some areas in your life where you could benefit from being more observant?

What sensory experiences do you find particularly captivating?

What biases or assumptions might be influencing your observations?

How can you incorporate mindfulness and active attention into your daily routine?

Tasks for Practice:

Choose an object you encounter routinely and observe it with concentrated attention for five minutes, noting every detail you can perceive.

Spend an hour in a public space, attentively listening to the conversations and noises around you. Try to discern the emotions and intentions behind the statements.

Observe a social interaction between two individuals. Pay close attention to their body language, facial expressions, and tone of voice. What can you deduce about their relationship and the dynamics at play?

Mastering the discipline of observation is a lifelong endeavor. It requires dedication, practice, and a willingness to see the world with new eyes. But the rewards are immense. By refining this skill, we become empowered to navigate the complexities of life with greater clarity, purpose, and pleasure.

Chapter 9: The Power of Questioning and Curiosity

Curiosity, the innate drive to learn and investigate, is the spark that ignites the fire of human potential. It propels us beyond the familiar, encouraging us to question the world around us and pursue deeper understanding. When coupled with the potent instrument of questioning, this insatiable curiosity becomes the propelling force behind our growth, innovation, and fulfillment.

Imagine a child encountering a novel object for the first time. Their eyes gleam with amazement as they bombard you with questions: "What is it?" "How does it work?" "Why is it shaped that way?" This relentless inquiry isn't just an innocent quirk; it is the natural manifestation of a curious mind actively pursuing knowledge and comprehension.

As we mature, however, the flame of inquiry often dims. We become conditioned to accept things at face value, to follow established norms, and to suppress the urge to query the status quo. This can contribute to stagnation, a lack of intellectual development, and a sense of disengagement from the world around us.

Fortunately, we can rekindle the flame of curiosity and harness the power of questioning to unlock our full potential. **Here are some ways to cultivate this powerful force:**

Embrace a Beginner's Mind:

Approach the universe with the open-mindedness and inquisitiveness of a child.

View everyday experiences as opportunities for learning and discovery.

Be willing to challenge your assumptions and contemplate alternative perspectives.

Ask Powerful Questions:

Don't settle for superficial responses. Dig deeper with probing queries that get to the core of the matter.

Ask "why" and "how" queries to uncover concealed causes and mechanisms.

Formulate open-ended queries that encourage discussion, debate, and innovative solutions.

Seek Diverse Perspectives:

Surround yourself with people who have various origins, experiences, and viewpoints.

Engage in frank and respectful dialogue, actively listening to their perspectives and challenging your own.

Consider and analyze information from numerous sources to broaden your understanding.

Practice Active Learning:

Move beyond passive absorption of information. Engage with the material by asking questions, taking notes, and summarizing the key points.

Apply your knowledge to real-world situations and solve problems creatively.

Share your insights and learnings with others, fostering a collaborative learning environment.

Embrace Uncertainty:

Don't be afraid of the unknown or the distress of not having all the answers.

View uncertainty as an opportunity for exploration, discovery, and personal growth.

Learn to be comfortable with ambiguity and embrace the process of pursuing answers.

Examples of Practical Steps To Guide You

Practice Daily Curiosity: Start with the mundane: Pick a commonplace object and spend a few minutes asking yourself questions about it. What is it composed of? How does it work? What purpose does it serve?

Embrace the "five whys": When confronted with a dilemma or challenge, ask yourself "why" five times. This helps you drill down to the fundamental cause and uncover concealed assumptions.

Question your routine: Challenge the way you do things every day. Ask yourself if there's a better, more efficient, or more pleasurable way to execute tasks.

Foster Question-Based Conversations:

Ask open-ended questions: Instead of pursuing straightforward yes/no answers, encourage deeper dialogue with open-ended questions that spark conversation and debate.

Listen actively: Pay close attention to the answers you receive and ask follow-up questions to clarify and expound upon their meaning.

Respect diverse perspectives: Be open to various viewpoints and contemplate them with an open mind, even if they differ from your own.

Create a Questioning Environment:

Surround yourself with inquisitive people: Interact with individuals who share your passion for learning and exploration. Engage in stimulating conversations and challenge each other to think critically.

Join learning communities: Participate in book societies, online forums, or workshops focused on topics that stimulate your curiosity. This allows you to learn from others and broaden your knowledge base.

Expose yourself to diverse sources of information: Read books on various subjects, view documentaries, listen to recordings, and attend lectures on topics that interest you. This broadens your perspective and stimulates your thought process.

Apply Questioning to Problem-Solving:

Identify the problem clearly: Define the issue you're confronting in plain and concise terms.

Gather information: Research the problem and acquire relevant information from various sources.

Brainstorm solutions: Generate a range of potential solutions through individual ideation or group discussion.

Evaluate and refine: Analyze each solution critically, identify potential drawbacks and advantages, and refine your approach based on the evaluation.

Reflect and Adapt:

Take time for reflection: Regularly assess your progress and identify areas where you can improve your inquiry skills.

Seek feedback: Ask trusted friends, mentors, or colleagues for honest feedback on your ability to ask excellent questions and listen actively.

Be patient and persistent: Cultivating a questioning mindset takes time and effort. Be patient with yourself, celebrate your progress, and keep practicing refining your abilities.

Tasks for Practice:

Choose a topic you're intrigued about and spend an hour researching it, asking yourself questions as you go.

Interview with someone who holds a different opinion than you on a specific issue. Ask open-ended queries and actively listen to their perspective.

Identify a problem you're currently facing and implement the inquiry approach to generate creative solutions. Evaluate each solution and choose the best course of action.

By cultivating an inquiring mind and embracing the power of curiosity, we unleash a world of possibilities. We become perpetual learners, driven by a thirst for knowledge and understanding. We develop the ability to think critically, analyze information objectively, and solve complex problems creatively. Most importantly, we rediscover the pleasure of exploration, the thrill of discovery, and the unyielding passion for learning that fuels extraordinary personal and professional development.

Chapter 10: Critical Thinking: Cutting Through the Noise

In an era of information inundation and competing narratives, critical thinking has emerged as an essential life skill. It empowers us to navigate the complexities of the world, distinguish truth from falsehood, and make informed decisions that align with our values and objectives.

Imagine a detective sifting through a mountain of evidence, painstakingly separating fact from fiction. They analyze each bit of information, considering its source, context, and potential biases. This meticulous approach allows them to piece together the conundrum, identify the perpetrator, and ultimately bring justice to the fore.

Similarly, critical thinking equips us with the tools to become detectives in the information age. We learn to analyze information with skepticism, to identify logical fallacies and concealed agendas, and to draw reasoned conclusions based on evidence, not emotions or personal biases.

Here are some key aspects of critical thinking:

Question everything: Don't embrace information at face value. Ask yourself questions about the source, the purpose, and the evidence supporting the claims.

Identify assumptions: Recognize and challenge your assumptions, as well as those conveyed in the information you encounter.

Evaluate evidence: Analyze the evidence provided to support claims, considering its validity, reliability, and objectivity.

Recognize logical fallacies: Be aware of common fallacies in reasoning, such as ad hominem assaults, straw man arguments, and false analogies.

Consider alternative perspectives: Explore diverse viewpoints and contemplate how the information might be interpreted from other angles.

Draw reasoned conclusions: Base your conclusions on evidence and logical reasoning, not emotions, biases, or wishful thinking.

Be receptive to new information: Remain flexible in your reasoning and be willing to modify your conclusions when presented with compelling new evidence.

By sharpening our critical thinking skills, we unlock a range of benefits:

Improved decision-making: We are better equipped to assess options, evaluate risks, and make informed choices that align with our values and objectives.

Enhanced problem-solving: We can approach challenges with a more analytical and objective perspective, leading to more effective solutions.

Reduced susceptibility to bias and manipulation: We become less vulnerable to misinformation, propaganda, and other forms of manipulation.

Greater intellectual curiosity: We cultivate a passion for learning and a desire to investigate new ideas and perspectives.

Increased self-awareness: We acquire a deeper understanding of our inclinations and limitations, allowing us to make more conscious and informed choices.

How To Put It Into Practical

Develop a questioning mindset:

Become an interrogator: Approach information with a healthy measure of skepticism. Ask queries about the source, the author's credentials, and the evidence presented.

Seek diverse perspectives: Read articles from various viewpoints, engage in debates with individuals who hold opposing opinions, and actively listen to their arguments.

Challenge your assumptions: Identify your own biases and preconceived notions. Ask yourself if they are influencing your interpretation of the information.

Practice analyzing information:

Identify essential arguments: When reading or listening to information, identify the primary points being made, and the evidence used to support them.

Evaluate the evidence: Analyze the validity of the evidence. Is it reliable? Is it objective? Is it pertinent to the argument being made?

Consider alternative explanations: Are there other methods to interpret the information? Are there other factors that may be contributing to the situation?

Recognize logical fallacies:

Familiarize yourself with common fallacies: Learn to identify fallacies such as ad hominem assaults, straw man arguments, and appeals to emotion.

Be on the alert for manipulative techniques: Watch out for emotionally charged language, laden words, and appeals to fear or urgency.

Evaluate arguments based on their logic, not their **emotional appeal:** Don't let yourself be persuaded by persuasive language or personal assaults.

 Develop your investigating skills:

Learn to use credible sources: Understand the difference between reputable and unreliable sources. Use academic journals, peer-reviewed articles, and government websites for accurate information.

Fact-check information: Verify information to be sure before sharing it with others. Use online fact-checking websites and cross-reference information with other sources.

Consider the context: Analyze information within the context in which it was presented. Be aware of the author's purpose and the intended audience.

Cultivate a growth mindset:

Embrace challenges: View learning as a continuous process. Be willing to confess when you're wrong and learn from your errors.

Seek feedback: Ask others for feedback on your critical thinking abilities. Identify areas where you can develop and be open to constructive criticism.

Stay curious: Maintain a lifelong inquiry about the world around you. Ask queries, seek out new information, and challenge yourself to think in new ways.

Questions for reflection:

In what aspects of your life do you struggle with critical thinking?

How can you become more adept at identifying logical fallacies in the information you encounter?

What steps can you take to verify information before sharing it with others?

How can you cultivate a growth mindset and embrace continuous learning?

Tasks for Practice:

Choose an article on a controversial topic and analyze it critically, identifying the arguments, evidence, potential biases, and logical fallacies.

Participate in a debate on a current issue. Research both sides of the argument and present your position plainly and logically.

Create a fact-checking checklist to help you evaluate the information you encounter online. Use this checklist to assess the credibility of news articles, social media posts, and other online content.

Critical thinking is not a static talent; it's a continuous process of learning and refinement. By actively engaging with information, challenging assumptions, and pursuing diverse perspectives, we cultivate a more open, informed, and resilient mind

PART 4: TRANSFORMING ORDINARY MOMENTS INTO EXTRAORDINARY RESULTS

Chapter 11: Decision-Making: From Impulse to Insight

The quality of our existence is directly bound to the quality of our decisions. Each choice, large or small, molds our experiences, defines our relationships, and ultimately determines our trajectory. Yet, in the face of incessant choices, from the quotidian to the momentous, we often find ourselves navigating a perilous terrain of impulses, emotions, and conflicting information.

Imagine an accomplished chess player contemplating their next move. They meticulously analyze the board, deliberating each prospective move and its consequences. They assess risks and rewards, anticipate their opponent's strategies, and ultimately make a calculated decision that sets them on the path to victory.

Similarly, we must approach decision-making with a strategic mindset. By transitioning from impetuous reactions to discerning choices, we unleash the power to create extraordinary outcomes in our lives.

Here are some key steps to move from impulse to insight in your decision-making:

Cultivate self-awareness:

Identify your triggers: Recognize the emotions, situations, or individuals that tend to provoke impulsive decisions.

Understand your values and priorities: Define what matters most to you and ensure your decisions align with those values.

Acknowledge your biases: Recognize your own biases and preconceived notions that may influence your choices.

Gather information:

Research and compile facts: Don't rely solely on intuitive sentiments or limited information. Seek diverse perspectives and acquire data to make informed decisions.

Consider alternative options: Don't hurry to the first solution that leaps to mind. Explore all available options and evaluate their pros and cons.

Seek advice from trusted sources: Consult with mentors, colleagues, or professionals for their insights and perspectives.

Evaluate your options rationally:

Identify the potential consequences: Consider the short-term and long-term implications of each choice. Analyze potential hazards and rewards.

Use logic and reason: Set emotions aside and focus on evaluating each option based on its merits and alignment with your objectives.

Apply decision-making frameworks: Utilize decision-making models such as cost-benefit analysis or SWOT analysis to structure your evaluation.

Make a conscious choice:

Don't rush: Take your time and avoid making impetuous decisions under duress.

Own your choice: Be confident in your decision and assume responsibility for its outcome.

Be flexible and adaptable: Be prepared to adjust your course of action if necessary based on new information or unforeseen circumstances.

Learn from your experiences:

Reflect on your past decisions: Analyze what worked well and what could have been enhanced.

Identify patterns and recurring challenges: Learn from your errors and develop strategies to avoid repeating them.

Continuously enhance your decision-making skills: Seek opportunities to learn and develop, read books on decision-making, and attend seminars or courses.

Questions For Reflection:

What are some situations where you tend to make impetuous decisions?

How can you best align your decisions with your values and priorities?

What are some tools and resources you can utilize to enhance your decision-making skills?

How can you learn from past decisions to make wiser choices in the future?

Tasks for Practice:

Identify an impending decision you need to make. Apply the decision-making frameworks discussed in this chapter

By mastering the art of decision-making, we acquire the power to shape our destinies with purpose and intention. We become architects of our own lives, capable of navigating challenges, grasping opportunities, and creating a future aligned with our aspirations.

Chapter 12: Taking Action: The Bridge Between Thought and Reality

Ideas, plans, and aspirations have the potential to transform our lives, but only when they are translated into action. Taking action is the bridge that connects the world of thought and the world of reality, the catalyst that converts potential into achievement.

Imagine a builder with a blueprint for a majestic structure. Yet, all the intricate details and meticulous calculations remain nothing more than possibilities until the first brick is set. It's through the act of taking action, of setting the plan into motion, that the vision becomes a tangible reality.

Similarly, we all possess within us the potential for extraordinary outcomes. We conceive concepts, formulate plans, and harbor fantasies of a brighter future. However, without the bridge of action, these aspirations remain confined to the domain of imagination.

Taking action is not merely about doing something; it's about doing something with intention and purpose. It's about aligning our actions with our objectives, values, and aspirations. It's about embracing the journey of progress, with its moments of struggle and triumph, and ultimately experiencing the gratification of bringing our aspirations to life.

Here are some key steps for building the bridge between thought and reality:

Cultivate a "can-do" mindset:

Embrace challenges: View obstacles as opportunities for development and learning.

Focus on progress, not perfection: Don't be hesitant to take the first step, even if you don't have all the answers.

Develop self-efficacy: Believe in your ability to attain your desired outcomes.

Translate goals into action steps:

Break down your objectives into manageable steps: This makes them less daunting and simpler to tackle.

Set realistic deadlines: Hold yourself accountable by establishing realistic deadlines for each phase.

Prioritize your duties: Focus on the most essential tasks first and avoid procrastination.

Take consistent action:

Develop a daily action plan: Schedule specific duties for each day to ensure consistent progress.

Create a routine: Establish a consistent routine that supports your action plan.

Celebrate minor wins: Acknowledge and reward yourself for your accomplishments, no matter how small.

Embrace continuous learning:

Seek feedback and advice: Learn from others who have achieved similar objectives.

Read books and articles on personal development and productivity.

Attend seminars and courses to enhance your skills and knowledge.

Overcome obstacles and setbacks:

Anticipate challenges: Identify prospective obstacles and develop strategies to overcome them.

Develop resilience: Don't let setbacks discourage you. Learn from them and keep moving forward.

Seek support: Surround yourself with positive and affirming individuals who believe in you.

Real-World Scenarios:

Starting a business: Turning the concept of a business into a thriving venture requires consistent action. This involves market research, devising a business plan, securing funding, launching the business, and perpetually adapting to market conditions.

Improving your health: Achieving a healthier lifestyle requires taking action, such as setting fitness objectives, making dietary adjustments, developing an exercise regimen, and overcoming cravings and temptations.

Learning a new skill: Mastering a new skill demands dedication and consistent action. This involves setting learning objectives, creating a study plan, practicing routinely, seeking feedback and guidance, and remaining patient throughout the learning process.

These scenarios illustrate the power of taking action in various aspects of life. By consistently taking action, we can transform our aspirations into tangible outcomes and experience the pleasure and satisfaction of achieving our objectives.

Questions for Reflection:

What are your greatest obstacles to taking action?

How can you cultivate a firmer "can-do" mindset?

What measures can you take today to advance closer to your goals?

How can you create a support system that encourages you to take action?

Tasks for Practice:

Choose one objective you want to attain and break it down into three actionable steps. Schedule these measures into your calendar and commit to taking them.

Identify one obstacle that prevents you from taking action and devise strategies to overcome it.

Share your aims and aspirations with a trusted acquaintance or family member. Ask them to hold you accountable and provide support as you work towards your objectives.

By taking action, we unleash the boundless potential that resides within each of us. We transform our aspirations into reality, construct meaningful lives, and leave a lasting impact on the world around us. Remember, the bridge between thought and reality is built one action step at a time. So, take the first step today and embark on the extraordinary voyage of transforming your aspirations into reality.

Conclusion: Embracing the Extraordinary

As you voyage through the pages of this book, you've encountered powerful principles and practical strategies designed to unlock the extraordinary potential within you. You've explored the transformative power of asking questions, adopted the art of cultivating a growth mindset, and discovered the keys to effective time management and goal setting.

But the genuine voyage begins now. The knowledge and insights you've gained are seedlings waiting to be planted in the fertile ground of your existence. It's time to take action, transmute inspiration into tangible results, and witness the extraordinary unfold.

Remember, the extraordinary doesn't exist in a distant, unattainable domain. It's woven into the fabric of our everyday experiences. It's in the silent moments of self-reflection, the persistent pursuit of development, and the courageous steps we take outside our comfort zones.

Embrace the extraordinary not as a destination, but as a means of being. Let inquiry be your compass, resilience your fortification, and self-belief your guiding light. Ask questions that inspire inquiry and challenge assumptions. Cultivate a mindset that sees possibilities where others see limitations. Take action, one step at a time, with unwavering commitment to your objectives and unwavering faith in yourself.

This is not the conclusion of your voyage, but rather the beginning of a remarkable adventure. As you embark on this extraordinary path, remember these words: Believe in yourself. Embrace the uncertain. Never cease learning. And above all, never give up on the extraordinary within you.

May your journey be filled with astonishment, purpose, and the pleasure of witnessing your extraordinary potential emerge into reality.

Epilogue

As an author and thought leader in the field of critical thinking, it is my sincere hope that Improves Clear Thinking: Turning Ordinary Moments into Extraordinary Results has provided you with the tools and knowledge necessary to enhance your cognitive abilities and achieve greater success in both your personal and professional life.

Throughout the book, we explored the value of clear thinking, the science behind it, and the practical ways in which you can improve your critical thinking skills. By learning how to approach problems systematically, spot biases, and think creatively, you can begin to turn everyday moments into extraordinary results.

While the road to improving your thinking may not always be easy, it is definitely worth it. With the right mindset, help, and practice, you can develop the skills necessary to navigate complicated situations with ease and make sound choices that positively impact your life and the lives of those around you.

I want to thank you for taking the time to read this book, and I hope that the information you have gained will serve you well throughout your journey to becoming a better, more critical thinker. Remember, the power to achieve amazing results is within your grasp.